MW01258855

JIMBO
ADVENTURES IN PARADISE

GARY PANTER

EDITED & DESIGNED BY ART SPIEGELMAN & FRANÇOISE MOULY

A RAW / 🏛 PANTHEON BOOK

Hi! BEANY, Hi!

MANY OF THESE CARTOONS FIRST APPEARED IN RAW MAGAZINE.

Library of Congress Cataloging-in-Publication Data

PANTER, GARY.
    Jimbo

    I. Title.
PN6727.P36J5 1988   741.5'973   87-46067

First Edition

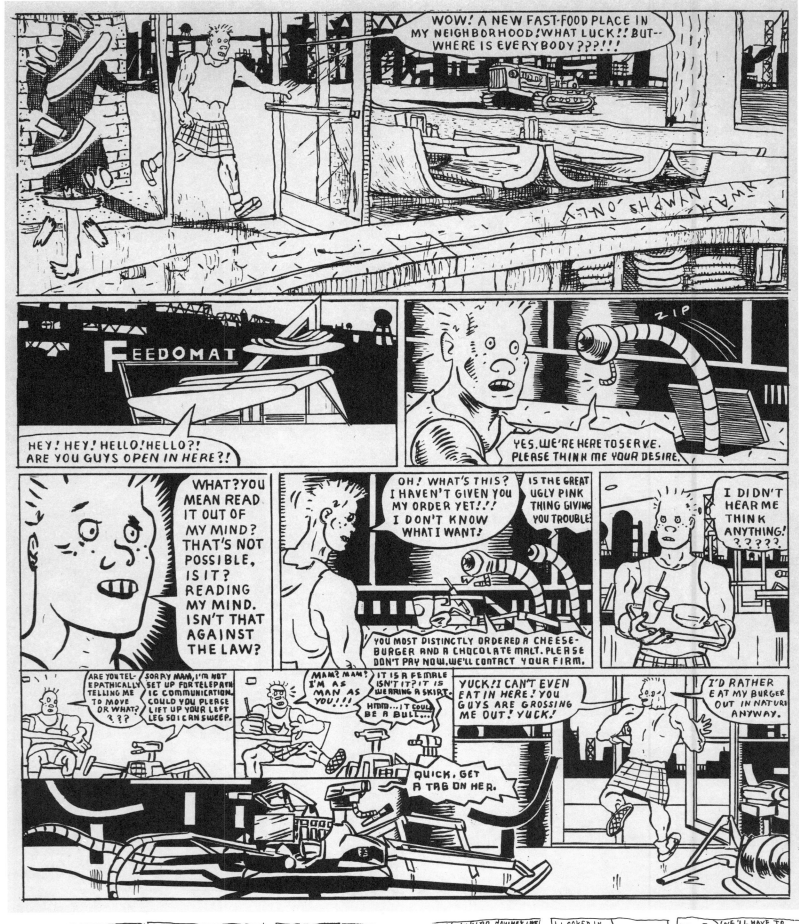

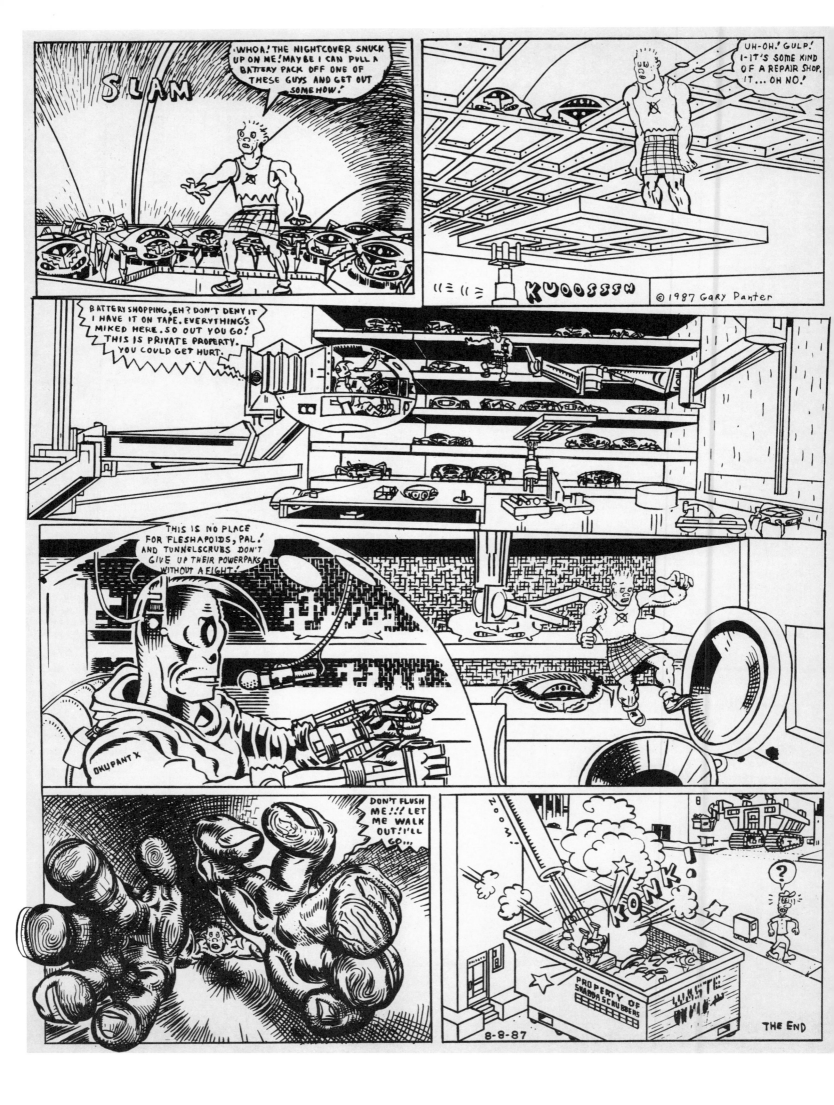

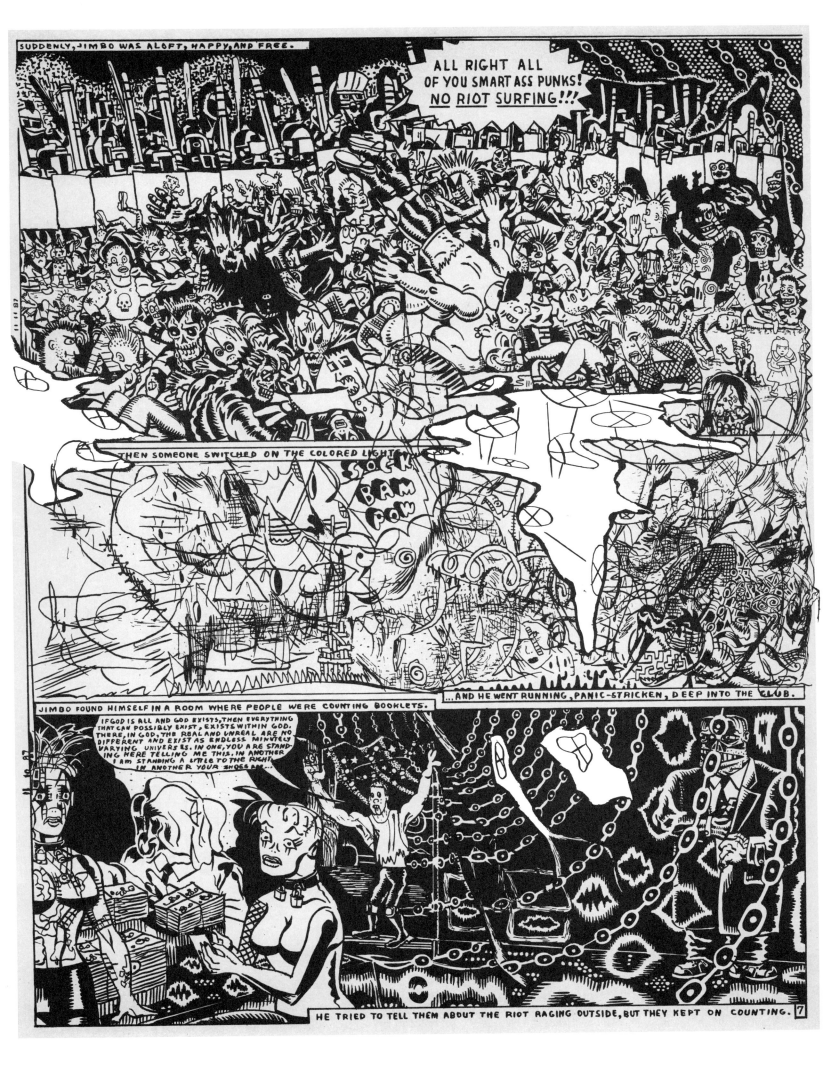

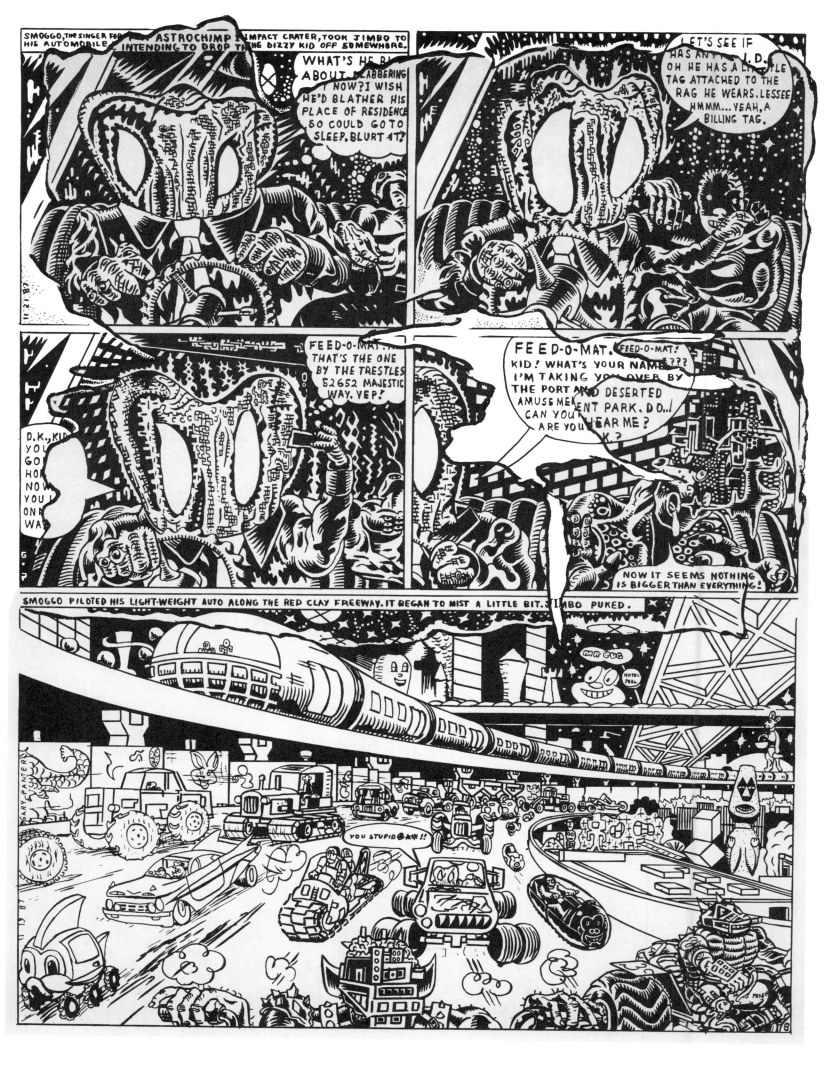

KZOW!

TALKIN' ABOUT PR...MAGE!

JIMBO RAN INTO THE KITCHEN AND DUCKED BEHIND AN ELECTRIC JUMBO MIXER. THE MECHANICAL SECURITY FORCE PURSUED HIM DISCHARGING BOLTS OF ELECTRICITY.

KEEP AWAY FROM ME WITH THAT IRON CLAW!

!!!

ON

OFF

HERE'S A PERFECT EXAMPLE OF A SITUATION WHERE MY BEST JUDGEMENT, AND REACTION TIME ARE JUST NOT FAST ENOUGH TO SAVE ME! I NEED BONLUCK. I NEED DUMB LUCK OF THE UNBELIEV...

THE THE ROBOT'S TENTACLE, TANGLED IN THE SPINNING MIXER BLADES, WAS INSTANTLY REELED IN LIKE A FISH AND RIPPED FROM ITS CEILING MOUNTS. PARTS REBOUNDING FROM THE HARD STEEL FLOOR COLLIDED WITH PARTS STILL RAINING DOWN.

SPANG
ZZZZZWWWW...
TCHOCK
WWWEEEE!
CLANK
CLANG
CLATTER

JIMBO WATCHED DEBRIS STILL TANGLED ON THE BLADES SHRED EVERYTHING IT TOUCHED IN THE AIR. THINGS FLEW BY TOO FAST FOR HIM TO THINK ABOUT DODGING. JIMBO WATCHED HIS DUMB LUCK BOOM RIGHT PAST HIS HEAD.

11

JIMBO ERECTUS

JIMBO ERECTUS. Their feeding habits have been the subject of much speculation in the past, but it is now Reliably known that they are mainly Predaceous.

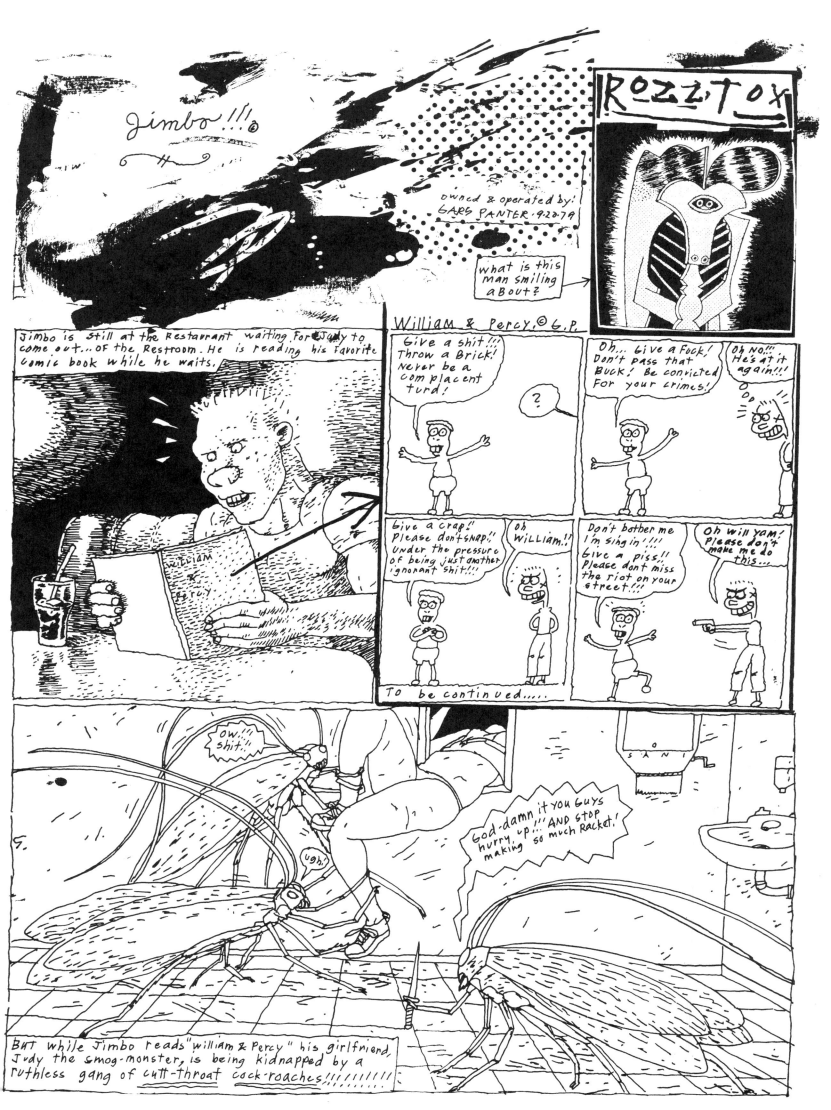

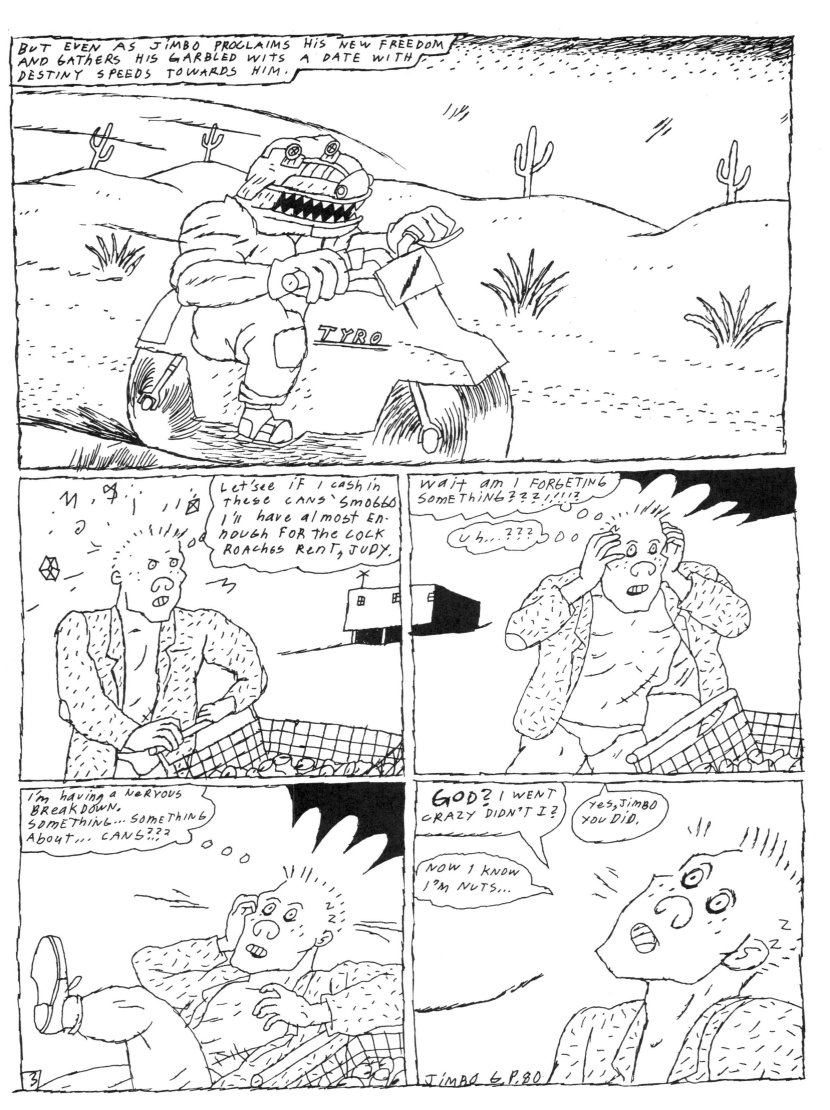

ONE MORNING WHEN THE COCKROACHES GOT UP THEY FOUND SMOGGO GONE. IT SCARED THE SHIT OUT OF THEM. THEY MARVELED THAT THEY HAD NOT BEEN MURDERED IN THEIR SLEEP. FEARING FOR THEIR CHITINOUS COVERINGS, THEY PACKED IN HASTE AND LEFT THE HIDE-OUT TAKING WITH THEM THE BOUND, BUT INCENDIARY, JUDY. AS THE OLD CHRYSLER BANGED OVER DESERT POTHOLES, THE SMOGETTE CAME TO THE END OF HER PATIENTLY PLAYED LINE.

MANY ANIMALS HAVE CLEVER NATURAL MEANS OF DEFENSE.

FOR THE SMŌGONS THE GOD-GIVEN DEFENSE IS FUSION.

A THOUSAND JUDIES GROW OUT OF THE RUBBLE AND MARCH OFF IN SEARCH OF JIMBO. A THOUSAND JUDIES. MAY 7 1982

THE ANNUAL PARADE of the followers of VEX PROHIAS, the nown invalid, rhythmically stomp down the street that run below the building in which JIMBO attempts the impossible.

The revelers are, of course, unaware that their pomp and circumstantial procession may soon be reduced to glowing ashes and blaring headlines.

3

"Can you prevent the bomb from going off?"

"No... I can not."

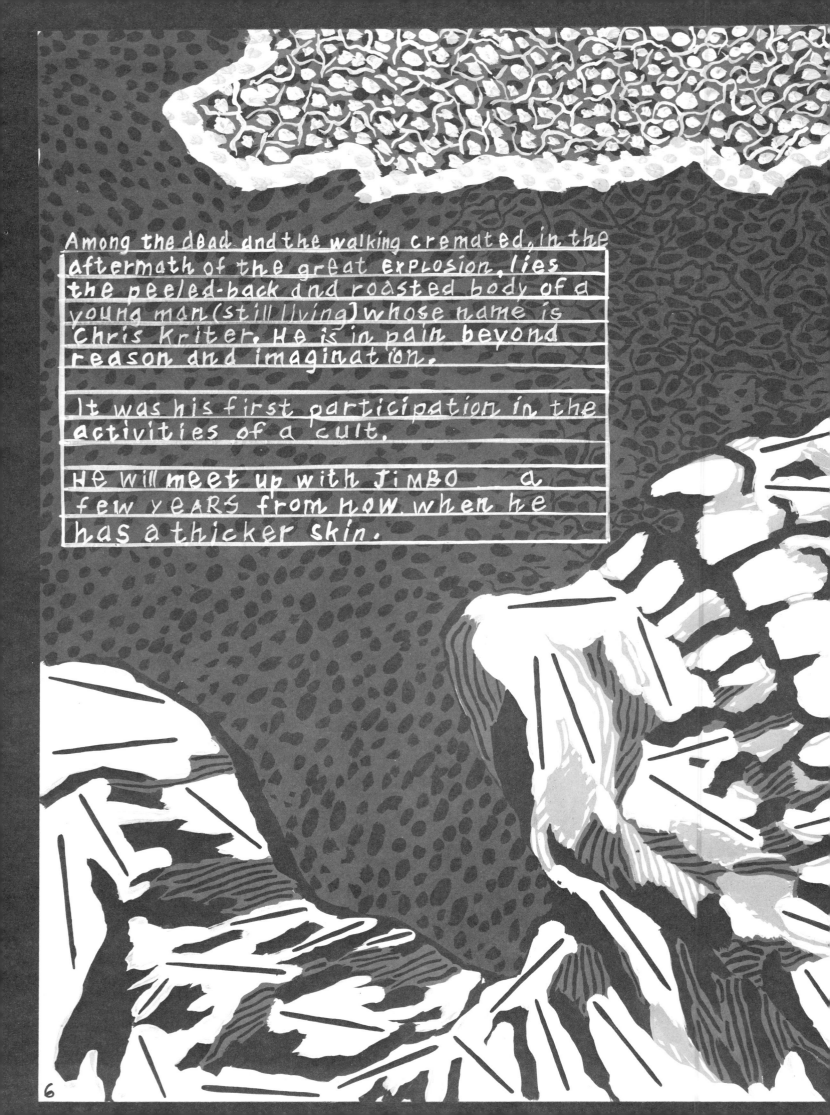

Among the dead and the walking cremated, in the aftermath of the great explosion, lies the peeled-back and roasted body of a young man (still living) whose name is Chris Kriter. He is in pain beyond reason and imagination.

It was his first participation in the activities of a cult.

He will meet up with JIMBO a few years from now when he has a thicker skin.

THE DOCTORS WILL BE COMING; IT PROBRABLY ONLY GOT FORTY MILES AROUND.

...COMING BECAUSE IT ONLY PROBRABLY GOT FORTY MILES AROUND.

3. THE FUNERAL DIRECTORS WILL BECOMING IN THEIR BLACK LIMOUSINES

WHEN WE DIE, things eat us UP; SO WE GO BACK FASTER. VULTURES.

at FIRST he thought they were monsters... then he thought they were afraid or wanted to come with him

JIMBO COULD SEE IT WAS NOT A SOUND MADE BY THE BABIES.

AAAAAAAAAAA

THE SOUND WAS AN OLD WHEEL SPINNING OUT BACK.

SaD BECAUSE IT WAS LIKE A CHEAP LITTLE SPOOK HOUSE, AN AMUSEMENT-

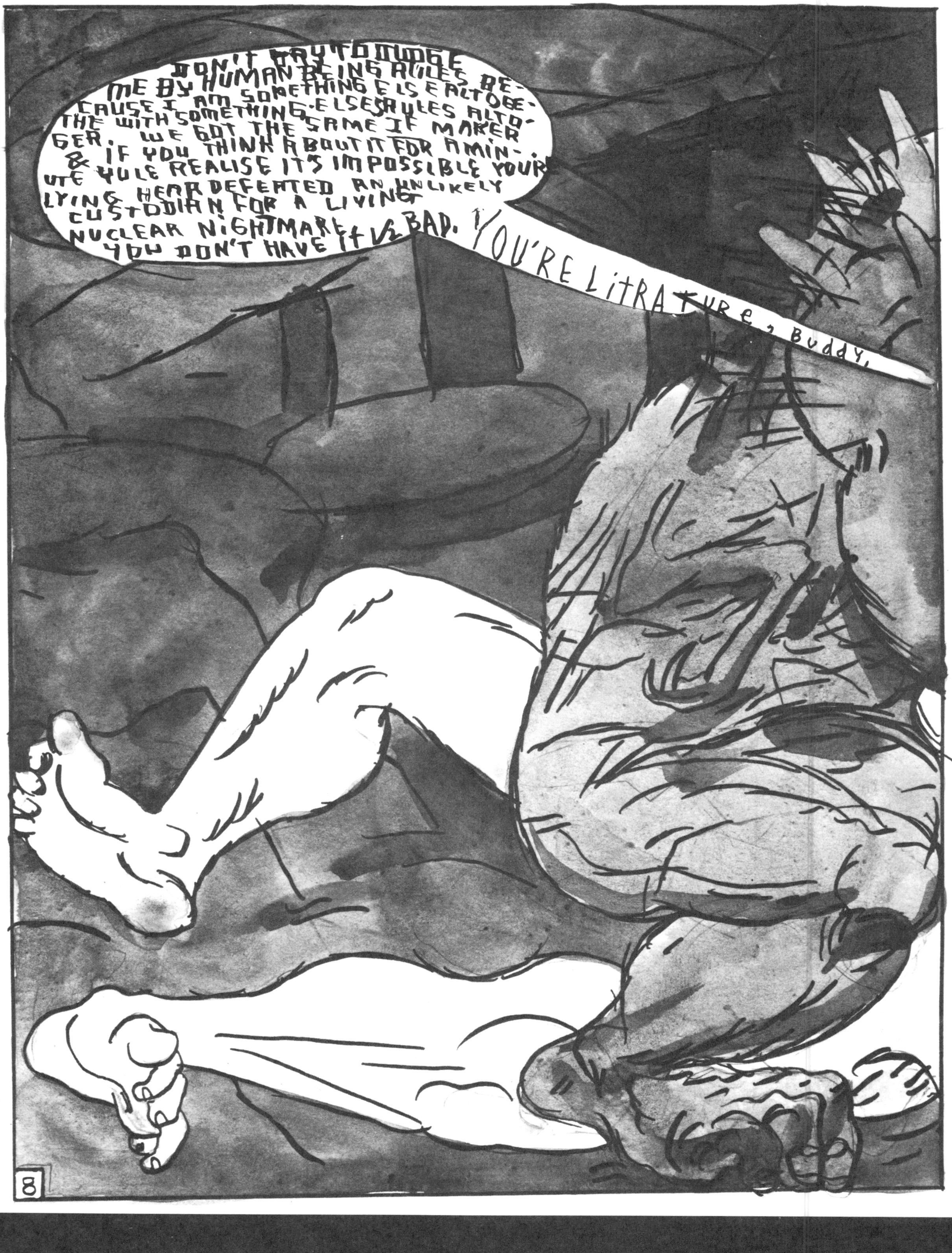

JIMBO

JIMBO IS STEPPING OFF THE EDGE OF A CLIFF!
What does it matter? He already is Bar-B-Qued and in the middle of a section of Dal-Tokyo destroyed by a small homemade terrorist A-bomb. All is ashes and carnage. The best aspect of the situation for Jimbo is that he doesn't feel guilty. Well, maybe a little. He didn't stop the bomb from going off, but he tried. He didn't make a career out of it or anything, but he was guileless. He didn't not let it go off on purpose. Sort of a blameless feeling anyway. Well, paying it off in the currency of the gods.
  He feels at least that nothing could be worse, that this is the bottom.
  Running barefoot on fire with his clothes melted off.
Pulverised. Pure.

DEC - 1 1985

Perhaps there is no... ... experiential Bottom

JimBo, as projectile, smashed into a pile of blazing jackstraws, unfettering anoth...

unfortunate: a horse.